LAURA INGALLS WILDER
GROWING UP IN THE LITTLE HOUSE

The Women of Our Time™ *series*
DOROTHEA LANGE: *Life Through the Camera*
BABE DIDRIKSON: *Athlete of the Century*
ELEANOR ROOSEVELT: *First Lady of the World*
DIANA ROSS: Star Supreme
BETTY FRIEDAN: *A Voice for Women's Rights*
MARGARET THATCHER: *Britain's "Iron Lady"*
DOLLY PARTON: *Country Goin' to Town*
OUR GOLDA: *The Story of Golda Meir*
MARTINA NAVRATILOVA: *Tennis Power*
MOTHER TERESA: *Sister to the Poor*
WINNIE MANDELA: *The Soul of South Africa*
GRANDMA MOSES: *Painter of Rural America*
MARY McLEOD BETHUNE: *Voice of Black Hope*
MARGARET MEAD: *The World Was Her Family*
LAURA INGALLS WILDER: *Growing Up in the Little House*

LAURA INGALLS WILDER

GROWING UP IN THE LITTLE HOUSE

BY PATRICIA REILLY GIFF
Illustrated by Eileen McKeating

VIKING KESTREL

*With love
to my own half-pint
Alice*

*A special thank-you to
Stell Garitz and Mary Alice Parmley*

VIKING KESTREL
Viking Penguin Inc., 40 West 23rd Street, New York, New York 10010, U.S.A.
Penguin Books Ltd, Harmondsworth, Middlesex, England
Penguin Books Australia Ltd, Ringwood, Victoria, Australia
Penguin Books Canada Limited, 2801 John Street, Markham, Ontario, Canada L3R 1B4
Penguin Books (N.Z.) Ltd, 182–190 Wairau Road, Auckland 10, New Zealand

Text copyright © Patricia Reilly Giff, 1987
Illustrations copyright © Eileen McKeating, 1987
All rights reserved
First published in 1987 by Viking Penguin Inc.
Published simultaneously in Canada
"Women of Our Time" is a trademark of Viking Penguin Inc.
Printed in the United States of America by Haddon Craftsmen,
Bloomsburg, Pennsylvania
Set in Garamond #3
1   2   3   4   5   91   90   89   88   87

Library of Congress Cataloging in Publication Data
Giff, Patricia Reilly.   Laura Ingalls Wilder: growing up in the little house.
(Women of our time)
Summary: A biography of the author of the "Little House" books,
including the years of her marriage to Almanzo Wilder.
1. Wilder, Laura Ingalls, 1867–1957—Biography—
Juvenile literature.   2. Authors, American—20th century—
Biography—Juvenile literature.   3. Children's stories—
Authorship—Juvenile literature.   4. Frontier and pioneer life—
Juvenile literature.   [1. Wilder, Laura Ingalls, 1867–1957.
2. Authors, American]   I. McKeating, Eileen, ill.
II. Title.   III. Series.   PS3545.I342Z65
1987   813'.52 [B] [92] 86-28202   ISBN 0-670-81072-X

CONTENTS

LAURA INGALLS WILDER
GROWING UP IN THE LITTLE HOUSE

1

The Little House

From the kitchen window Laura could look out at their farm, Rocky Ridge. The trees she and Manly had planted spread shady patches across the lawn. Beyond them, the crops were planted in even rows.

Soon the vegetables would be ready—fat red potatoes, plump beans, curly-headed cabbages, rich earth still clinging to them. Some would be sold, others stored away for the winter.

Inside, the house smelled of the sweet jam she had poured into jars; the pickles, the corn relish.

It was a busy time for Laura, a hard time, but life on a farm was like that.

Hard? How her father, Pa, would have laughed.

Hard was tracking through knee-deep snow for three days to catch a bear for food, he'd tell her.

Hard was being huddled in a cabin around a fire as snow and wind raged across the prairie.

Hard was a cloud of grasshoppers, the noise of their chewing filling the air as they ate every leaf, every stem of the precious food Pa had planted.

Laura looked out at the road that ran past the farm. Cars traveled along it, and trucks. She and Manly had their own Chrysler in the garage, and wonderful farm machines in the barn—things Pa hadn't even heard of.

Now telephone wires looped across the country; a radio on her kitchen shelf brought company into the house all day long—stories and songs and news.

Hard? Yes, Pa would have laughed.

Pa's life had been really hard, but Laura could remember that he had laughed often, a big hearty roar of a laugh that made all of them laugh with him.

She thought about the stories he had told, the games he had played. He'd crawl on the floor with her and her sister Mary on his back, his hair all "woozled up," pretending he was a bear.

Most of all she remembered the fiddle. After supper Pa would tuck it under his arm to play. As the firelight made the cabin glow, he'd tap his feet and

4

sing the songs they loved in his loud, deep voice.

That was so long ago, back in the 1800s when she was a little girl. Her hair had hung down her back in two tight braids. She remembered begging until her mother let her cut a little fringe of bangs across her forehead.

Now, in the window's reflection, she stood as straight as she could. Only five feet tall, she always tried to make herself seem taller. Her eyes were violet blue. Her hair was white and curled around her face. It was 1930. She was sixty-three years old.

Almost no one could remember the old days anymore. When she was gone, no one would know about Pa's life, or his stories, or that he had called her "Little Half-Pint of Cider Half Drunk Up."

Even her daughter Rose, Pa's grandchild, wouldn't know.

Standing there, Laura thought about it. When Rose was little, she'd say, "Oh tell me another, Mama! Please tell another story!"

That's what she'd do. She'd write down some of the old stories for Rose.

Rose was far away in New York now, a well-known writer and journalist. She had written many pioneer stories for magazines, and Laura's writing might even help Rose add some interesting facts to her stories.

Laura loved to write, anyway. She wrote often for

farm magazines and the *Missouri Ruralist* newspaper. She thought of writing as painting pictures with words. "The only stupid thing about words," she said, "is the spelling of them."

As soon as she had a few minutes to spare, Laura went to her little study and opened the drop-leaf desk Manly had made for her when they were first married. She fished around for a pencil and pulled out a lined yellow pad. She was ready to begin.

She reached back in her mind, back as far as she could remember, and then further, to what her mother and father had told her about the Big Woods. It would be a good place to begin, because Rose had said she had never "lost my very-little-girl feeling that the Big Woods was somewhere in fairyland or at least what was the same region, my mother's when-I-was-a-little-girl time."

Laura began her book. "Once upon a time, sixty years ago," she wrote across the pad, "a little girl lived in the Big Woods of Wisconsin, in a little gray house made of logs."

Laura was the little girl, of course, and her house was the house where she had been born, in 1867.

That winter two giant oak trees stood guard over the little house in the Wisconsin woods. Today the house has crumbled away and even most of the Big Woods has been cut down. Lake Pepin is still there, though, and nearby there's a marker to show that Laura and her family once lived there.

It was freezing cold in February that year. A horse and carriage could be driven safely across the ice on the lake. In the woods the evergreens were thick with caps of snow.

Inside the house Charles and Caroline Ingalls were waiting. Their second baby was coming.

Charles, a farmer, a trapper, was a man who had very little schooling. He loved people. His wife, Caroline, was a fine, quiet woman. She loved books and writing and had been a schoolteacher before she was married.

The baby, a girl, was born on February 7, 1867. Her mother decided to name her Laura Elizabeth. Her father would call her Half-Pint. She would be good company for her two-year-old sister, Mary.

Laura would live in that little house twice, during her first year and again when she was three.

In between, the Ingalls family traveled in a covered wagon with a billowy white top through the rest of Wisconsin, south and west through Iowa, and into Missouri and Kansas.

Laura didn't want to tell about that trip in her book. She wanted to write about life in the little log house that Pa and Uncle Henry, Ma's brother, had built with their own hands. She wanted to tell today's children what it was like to be a child in America long ago.

Because she was so little when she lived in that house, she made herself a little older for the book, and Mary, too. Her little sister, Carrie, born in Kansas, was the baby. Laura wrote about Mary, her sister, who was neat and tidy. She spoke about herself the way she was, quick to speak, quick to move, never as neat as Mary, and wishing she had Mary's golden hair instead of her own plain brown. Sometimes she was angry with Mary, jealous, and once she slapped her. Instead of using *I* when she wrote about Laura, she used *she*. It seemed more like a story that way.

She painted word pictures of nights in that little house, when Pa, finished with his hunting and trapping, would sit by the fire, playing "Yankee Doodle" on his fiddle.

Next to him, Ma would finish darning and listen, smiling. Laura and Mary and Baby Carrie were tucked up tight under the bright quilts Ma had made for them. They were cozy, and safe from the wolves that roamed the woods outside.

Laura wrote about things that children didn't see now . . . how she and Mary played with a pig bladder blown up into a balloon . . . how Mary sewed a nine-patch quilt . . . how Ma made hats of yellow straw from the oats in the field.

Running through the book were Pa's stories, won-

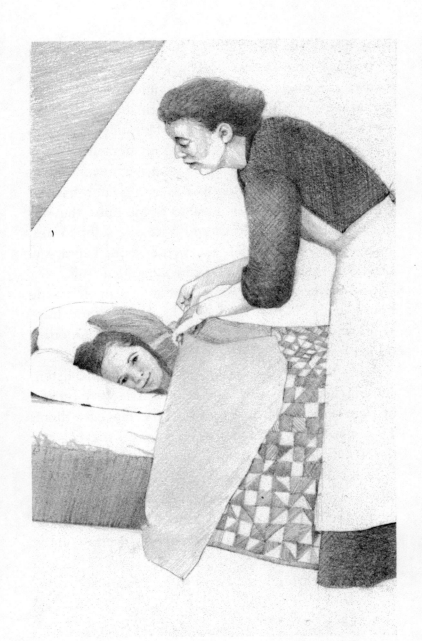

derful stories, old stories. He told of the panther chasing Grandpa through the woods, and how Grandpa slipped to safety through his cabin door at the very last minute. He told of being lost in the woods as a boy, thinking that wild animals were all around him.

Page after page of Laura's pad was filled. She sent off what she had written to Rose, calling it *When Grandma Was a Little Girl.*

Rose loved it. She knew an editor, who read it and enjoyed it, too. The editor wanted Laura to work on it a little more.

Laura went back to her study, back to the yellow lined paper, and added more stories, rounded out the ones she had.

At last it was finished. When she was sixty-five years old, in 1932, it was published. It had a new name, *The Little House in the Big Woods.*

"It was a labor of love," Laura said, "a memorial to my father."

2

Manly

Now that her book was published, Laura went back to her work. With a large farm to look out for, there was always something that she and Manly had to do.

She didn't mind the outside work. She had always loved the outdoors, with the wide sky and the dark soil.

Cleaning was a different story. So was baking. Bread had to be made twice a week. It had to be kneaded, punched, set to rise, and baked—a job that took hours. How she hated it!

Manly had cut a huge window into the wall in front

of her kitchen counter. While she punched the bread, she could look out at their land and think her own thoughts.

After the pale round loaves had been set into pans and put at the back of the stove to rise, she would walk down to the hens.

By this time she was an expert on poultry. People in their town of Mansfield always said that she could coax eggs from her hens even in the winter, when most hens wouldn't lay for anyone else.

Since 1911, when she was forty-four, she'd been writing for two newspapers about the farm, and the hens, and other things that had to do with farm life. She had been the poultry editor of the *St. Louis Star* and the home editor of the *Missouri Ruralist*.

She was a little surprised that anyone would want to read her writing. "I never graduated from anything," she said, "and only attended high school two terms."

Laura hadn't settled back into farm life very long when something happened. What happened was that children discovered her book, *The Little House in the Big Woods*. They found it in libraries and bookstores. They told their friends about it. They read it a second time, even a third time. Grown-ups loved it, too. It was honored as a Junior Literary Guild book for 1932. The book was printed again and again.

"What do you think?" Laura asked. "Children who read it wrote to me begging for more. I was amazed because I didn't know how to write."

She went around the farm, doing her work, trying to decide what she could write next for the children who kept writing, kept asking.

Her thoughts went back to Manly. For forty-seven years he had been her husband. He was always there next to her. Sometimes she was a little sharp with him, sometimes impatient, but he was her whole life. Manly with his blue eyes, his soft mustache. Manly who loved horses and farming. Manly who had limped along with a cane since he was thirty years old because of that dreadful disease called diphtheria. Luckily it was a disease that people didn't get anymore because they were injected against it when they were babies.

She didn't like to think about Manly's diphtheria. It was more fun to think about the first time she had seen him. As usual, she had done something without thinking about it first. She had nearly gotten herself and her little sister Carrie into a dangerous situation.

It had started when Pa had asked her to go to town. He needed something from Fuller's hardware store. Quickly Laura had changed her dress and her shoes and begged Ma for her Sunday hair ribbon and Mary's ironed bonnet. Mary's bonnet was always fresh, and hers was a mess from hanging down her back. It was her own fault, her mother told her, and sent her off in her messy bonnet with Carrie.

On the way back, Laura decided she'd take Carrie home another way, a shortcut. This way went through the sough (say it like "sow"), a marshy land where tall grasses grew, grasses that waved in the breeze high over their heads.

In no time they were lost. They wandered through the sough, not able to see where they were. There was nothing to climb on, no way to tell if they were going in the right direction. Uneasily Laura remembered that Ma was always worried about that sough.

It was hot, Carrie was tired, and Laura was beginning to wonder if they'd wander around in there forever.

Then she heard a voice. "Get a move on, Manzo," it said.

Next Laura saw a wagon and a hayfield at the edge of the sough. Up on top was a boy. His blue eyes were dancing, he was laughing, and when he saw Laura, he called hello.

The boy, of course, was Manly.

She still smiled, thinking about it.

Yes, she'd write about Manly. Laura would make it the story of his life, growing up on a farm outside of the town of Malone, New York. It was a much different life than hers had been, farther west.

She set the time of the book around the year she was born, which made Manly almost ten years old.

When children read it, she thought, they'd be able to see how different life had been in the 1860s.

Manly's clothes came from their own sheep. Even the thread his mother used for sewing came from butternut hulls. She spent time dying the wool and the thread in different colors so her family would look well-dressed.

Manly had gone to a one-room school called the Skeelsboro School. Laura changed its name for the book to the Hardscrabble School, but she described it as it really was. "The girls sat on the left side of the room and the boys sat on the right side," she wrote, "with the big stove and woodbox in the middle between them."

She would tell about Manly's deep feeling for horses. He loved the way they looked, and he liked to think about what they could do for the farmer.

In the early 1900s he had realized that a new type of horse was needed for the Ozark area of Missouri where they lived then. This horse would have to be able to pick his way through stony fields; he would have to have a strong back to pull the heavy farm loads.

Manly had brought the first Morgan horse to the area, a horse named Governor of Orleans. Manly had been right. The Morgan was a wonderful horse, and his colts had been perfect for the rocky land of Missouri.

Laura called her book *Farmer Boy*. She sent it off to her publisher—who sent it right back. Laura would have to rewrite to make it good enough to publish. That year Laura spent every spare minute writing. She crossed out. She changed. Next year the book was back with the publisher, ready to go.

17

Again children were delighted. They loved Manly . . . how much he ate . . . how he loved horses.

Today Manly's house still stands in Malone, New York, although it is no longer owned by the Wilder family. The barns are gone, but Trout River flows nearby, as it did in the book. Horses and cows graze in the meadows, and wheat grows in the fields.

Life has changed. Bad boys don't learn to behave with a blacksnake whip such as Mr. Corse, the teacher, used. Clothing is bought, and big farms like the Wilders' use modern machinery.

By 1933 the postman arrived at Rocky Ridge Farm every day with letters. *Farmer Boy* was being read all over the country.

When was Mrs. Wilder going to write something else? What happened next to Laura? To Almanzo?

Laura thought about it. "I had seen the whole frontier," she said, "the woods, the Indian country, the frontier towns, the building of the railroads in wild, unsettled country, homesteading, and farmers coming in to take possession."

She decided she would write more books about that childhood, her growing-up years, and the time when she was first married. She wanted to tell children "what it is that made America as they know it."

3

Restless Feet

Laura planned to write eight books. The next six would tell about her life as a pioneer girl and then as a farmer's wife.

It was a lucky thing that Pa had "restless feet." At least that's what he called them. Those feet made pioneers of the Ingalls family.

They left the little house in Pepin, Wisconsin, to go across the country, from state to state. Next, they traveled to Indian Territory in Kansas. Then they spent time in Plum Creek and Walnut Creek, Minnesota, and in Burr Oak, Iowa. By 1879 they had settled in De Smet, South Dakota.

The Ingalls family wasn't alone. Those open lands were calling farmers from all over the East.

Best of all, so much of the land was free!

Homesteading was a wonderful new law set up by the government. All a man had to do was stake out a certain piece of land. He had to live on it and work it for five years. Then he'd receive a deed saying the land belonged to him completely.

Years later, when Laura sat down to write the *Little House* books, the memory of her trips was vivid to her. As the covered wagon had rocked along, she sat in the back to look out at the prairie. It was a vast flat land with golden grasses swaying gently on each side of the wagon for as far as she could see. Birds flew overhead, and jackrabbits scampered in front of them.

Sometimes it was exciting. Laura liked sleeping under the stars. It was fun to eat outside next to the wagon. Ma cooked bacon or beans, or pancakes in a spider— a little frying pan with legs.

It wasn't all easy. In *The Little House on the Prairie* she told of crossing the Missouri River. "Pa drove onto a raft, and . . . the raft went swaying away from the safe land and slowly crossed all that rolling muddy yellow water."

Most of the time it was too hot or too wet. When it rained, "there was no place to make camp and build a fire," Laura wrote. "Everything was chill and miserable in the wagon, but they had to stay in it and eat cold bits of food." There was no room. All they owned was jammed into every part of the wagon. The children had to stay inside with Ma. Pa sat outside, guiding the horses, the rain running off his hat.

Laura hated to sit still. She kept asking when they were going to get there. It was too hot, too long, too wet, she complained.

Her mother never raised her voice. Quietly she said, "Laura." That meant stop. That meant behave.

Laura wrote that "she did not complain anymore out loud, but she was still naughty inside. She sat and thought complaints to herself."

Homesteading was not as simple as people thought. Sometimes records were mixed up; sometimes the settlers weren't sure which piece of land belonged to which person.

In Kansas this happened to Pa. After a year of building and planting and working, he found they were living on Indian territory. They had to leave everything and move on.

To the Indians, homesteading certainly wasn't simple. The government was giving away some of their land. Even though they didn't have a paper saying so, all of it had belonged to them for hundreds of years.

The Indians were angry. Many of them couldn't

speak English so they couldn't make themselves understood. In some places, when settlers built cabins and began to plant, the Indians fought back. They burned cabins, they trampled land. People on both sides were killed.

One of Laura's earliest memories was about the Osage Indian Tribe. In *The Little House on the Prairie* she wrote about the huge powwow, or meeting, they held.

Group after group met at Drum Creek near the Ingalls cabin. For days the sounds of their drums echoed across the prairie.

Ma was frightened. Worse than that, she was terrified. If Pa had to leave her at night, she would sit in her rocker, waiting with his gun on her lap. Laura wanted to know more about what was happening, but "children should be seen and not heard," Ma always said. So Laura watched and worried, but she didn't ask too much.

The settlers went about their work, listening, wondering if there would be a war. One night the sounds of the Indians' cries grew fiercer. Every hour the beat of the drums was louder. The Ingalls stayed awake, huddled around the fire until daylight. Laura was terribly afraid. When night was over, Ma couldn't stop trembling.

There was no war. It was because of a special Indian

leader, Soldat du Chene. Pa had pointed him out to Laura. This leader calmed the Osages, warned them that they were outnumbered by the white men.

When the Indians left, Pa held Laura up to the little window in their cabin. She watched, as line after line of Osage Indians rode past and disappeared west across the prairie.

In Minnesota Laura saw her first sod houses. She

wrote about them in *On the Banks of Plum Creek*. Because there were so few trees on the prairie, settlers had to find something else for building material. They used the land itself, tough pieces of sod baked in the sun, which provided good strong walls and roofs.

The house they'd live in was the strangest of all, Laura thought. When she first saw it, she climbed down from the wagon to look at the creek. First she listened to the sound of the gurgling water. Then she noticed a door. "It stood straight up in the grass bank, where the path turned. It was like a house door, but whatever was behind it was under the ground."

Behind it, Laura soon found out, was a house, their house.

At first it seemed that they were alone on the prairie with only jackrabbits to keep them company. The first Sunday, Pa took them to church in Walnut Grove. Other settlers were there, and more were coming.

Not only was there a church, but in the spring a school was built. Ma was delighted. Her girls had to learn to read, had to be educated.

Laura wasn't so happy with school. She and Mary had to wear dresses that were too short. Their legs looked long and skinny, so the boys called them "snipes," those long-legged birds. She swung her lunch pail at them. "You all sound like a flock of prairie chickens!" she shouted.

Laura soon made friends with the boys. She found she didn't like the learning part as much as she liked playing ball with the boys at recess, or throwing snowballs in the wintertime. She liked to whistle, too. She could whistle as well as any of the boys. That wasn't ladylike at all.

Mary was horrified at her tomboy sister and told Ma.

Ma wasn't happy about that kind of behavior, either. Laura was in trouble. She had to learn to keep her bonnet on straight the way Mary did and to behave like a lady in school!

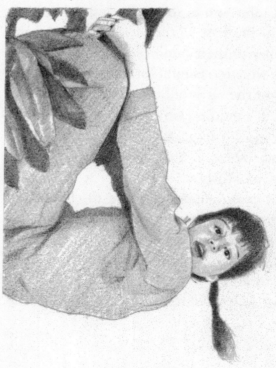

Life wouldn't run smoothly at Plum Creek. That summer, as the tender shoots of wheat struggled up through the soil, the sky darkened. It was a strange kind of dark, a greenish color. There were strange sounds, too—whirring, clicking, chomping. Grasshoppers, thousands, millions, hopping over the land, eating everything in their path.

Years later Laura said, "There are unforgettable pictures of those grasshoppers in my mind that I have tried to draw plainly in *On the Banks of Plum Creek.*"

Laura wrote about the grasshoppers. She wrote that the crops were gone, that there would be no money from the land. She wrote about Pa and other men walking miles to the East so they could find jobs and send back money to their families.

Other things were too painful for her to write about. She never told of the birth of little Charles Frederick, whom she called Freddie. Tiny and frail, he was her only brother, and he lived for nine months. "One awful day, he straightened out his little body and was dead," she said years later.

Sickness and death happened often to children in those days. There were no shots for measles and mumps. Few doctors lived within riding distance, and even when there was a doctor nearby, he didn't have modern medicines to help.

Laura told of Mary's blindness in *By the Shores of*

Silver Lake, but she told very little about how it had happened.

They had had scarlet fever, Ma and Mary and Carrie and even the little baby, Grace. Then one day Mary had a headache, a terrible pain. Her temperature kept going higher. Every day she was sicker. Desperately, they tried to bring her fever down. Ma even cut off Mary's long golden hair so she'd be cooler.

Laura remembered all the times she was angry because Mary had such beautiful hair. She remembered their arguments. Now she was afraid Mary would die.

"One morning when I looked at her," Laura said, "I saw one side of her face drawn out of shape. Ma said Mary had had a stroke."

The stroke affected her eyes. Little by little, her vision dimmed. "The last thing Mary ever saw," Laura said, "was the bright blue of Grace's eyes, as Grace stood holding the chair looking up at her."

Now Laura began to look at things differently. She had to study everything, find ways to put things into words. She wanted Mary to "see" them, too. Putting word pictures together for Mary probably helped Laura later when she began to write.

In the meantime Pa's feet were restless again. Aunt Docia, his sister, arrived with news that delighted him and made Ma sigh. How would they like to move to South Dakota? Aunt Docia wanted to know. Pa could work with Uncle Hiram, her husband, on the railroad. Tracks were being laid farther and farther West.

That night Pa's fiddle sang again. The songs were cheery and promising. Exciting days were coming.

Laura was excited, too. She thought about the covered wagon, the nights under the stars, the grasses swaying gently on the prairie. They'd be able to homestead again, and their wheat would come up green and strong. Pa would have money he'd earn working on the railroad.

Yes, they were off to the Dakotas, the very heart of the prairie.

4

Prairie Girl

In 1880 the frost came early to De Smet, South Dakota. Pa saw signs that pointed to a hard winter.

He showed thirteen-year-old Laura the muskrats' houses. They were thick this year, thick enough to protect the animals from cold and blizzards. He pointed to the birds overhead, all of them flying high and fast to leave the prairie.

Pa was uneasy. The temperature kept dropping. It was too cold to stay on the homestead claim in the little shanty made of pine wood. They'd have to live over a store in town for the winter.

This was the beginning of the time Laura would write about in *The Long Winter.*

School started. It came to an abrupt end a few weeks later in the middle of the afternoon. The sky grew slate gray, snow began to fall. Great white flakes covered the world and swirled in a blast of wind. The teacher, Miss Florence Garland, who was only eighteen years old herself, and her pupils had to find their way to their homes by holding on to each other and guessing the way. The storm was so bad that had they made a mistake, they might have been lost on the prairie and died in the blizzard.

The Ingalls family settled in for a long, hard winter. The snow kept coming. Day after day, white covered the land. Laura remembered, "Snowdrifts in one night were piled as high as the second stories of the houses and packed hard enough to drive over."

These drifts covered the railroad tracks. Trains couldn't bring food or supplies. Getting enough food would be a problem.

A greater problem was keeping warm. Trees around the lake were cut down. Neighbors moved in with each other, and houses were taken apart. Every single piece of wood was needed to burn for heat.

Laura made "cats" all day long. She'd take pieces of hay, braid them together, and twist them so they'd burn slowly enough in the stove to give off heat. Her

hands ached and even bled from working at them, but there was no other way. Nothing else was left for the fire that had to be kept alive.

Soon there was no sugar left in town. Worse, there was no wheat, and that meant no bread.

Manly rode across the prairie with a friend, between storms, to find wheat. They managed to find farmers miles away who were willing to share some supplies. Manly and his friend made it back with the wheat just before the next storm hit.

Laura thought winter would never end. She kept thinking about spring, when everything would be green. She waited to hear the sound of water trickling that would mean the snow had started to melt. It wasn't until March tenth that the first train made it through.

As the prairie came to life again and the wild roses Laura loved started to bloom, Pa and Ma talked to her about Mary. Mary needed to know as much as she could so she could take care of herself. If only she could be sent to the College for the Blind.

It would be hard to get enough money together, really hard. Would Laura be willing to help?

Gone was Laura's envy over Mary's golden hair. She knew how much she loved her sister. For six weeks that summer, she worked in Clayson's store, sewing. She hated making shirts and sewing on buttons, but she was happy to earn the dollar and a half a week. It was wonderful to give Mary nine dollars to help pay for school.

In September, when Mary left, the house seemed strange, lonesome. Laura studied harder. She was going to be a teacher like Ma. Sometimes she didn't think it would be so wonderful to teach. Everyone was always making fun of her own teacher, Liza Jane Wilder, who was Manly's sister. Laura had even written a poem about her:

> *Going to school is lots of fun*
> *By laughter we have gained a ton.*
> *For we laugh until we have a pain*
> *At lazy, lousy Liza Jane.*

No, Laura thought, teaching might be a miserable job.

She had the chance to find out before Christmas. Even though she wouldn't be sixteen until February, when most teaching licenses were given, Laura passed her tests and began to teach in December.

It was a scary feeling when Pa hitched up the wagon to drive her the fifteen miles to where she'd be teaching. She could remember how nervous she was, many years later, when she told about it in *These Happy Golden Years*. She was to stay with a family she called the Brewsters in the book.

Quickly she found out that Mrs. Brewster didn't

want her there. She was so unfriendly that after school Laura would go behind the curtain into the small area that held her bed to be by herself.

If only she could go home! How she missed Ma and Pa!

At school things were a little easier. Laura didn't mind teaching. Even though she was tiny, the big boys soon respected her, and all the children seemed to want to learn.

The first weekend came. Laura wondered how she'd get through it. Everything at the Brewsters' was so different from home, so cold, so silent.

Then she heard the tinkling of sleigh bells. It was Manly in a sled "so low and small that it was hardly more than a heap of furs on the snow behind Prince and Lady," the two horses.

Manly had known she'd be homesick. He'd driven across the frozen prairie to take her home for the weekend. Laura was overjoyed. After that he never missed a weekend, and even when her teaching time was up in the spring, Laura still took rides with him.

On one of the rides, when she was seventeen, Manly asked her to marry him. "He kissed me goodnight," she said, "and I went into the house not quite sure if I were engaged to Manly or to the starlight and the prairie."

A year later, on August 25, 1885, Laura put on the black cashmere wedding dress Ma had helped her make. It was beautiful, she thought, and would do nicely after the wedding for Sunday best. She and Manly drove alone to the preacher's homestead to be married. Laura made sure that Mr. Brown left out the word "obey." She had never liked that part.

At home her family waited, Ma bustling around to cook a wonderful noon dinner for the newlyweds. Then it was time for Laura to say good-bye. She clung to them at the door, then climbed up on the buggy for the short drive to her new house.

Laura wrote about her married life in *The First Four Years*. She wrote about funny things. Farmers had come to help Manly, and she was to feed them. Her beans turned out as hard as rocks, and she had forgotten to put sugar in the pie. How terrible she felt, and how angry at herself for being careless.

She wrote about the parts of her new life that she liked. Manly had bought her a gray pony named Trixy. She learned to ride so well that she even beat Manly in a race against his pony, Fly.

She wrote about some of the hard times, too. They had so little money. They had to count on the wheat Manly planted. Laura kept watching it grow—first little green shoots, then strong, sturdy, plants. The summer went on. Laura watched the wheat, watched the sky. Suppose there was a bad storm. Suppose . . .

She tried not to think about what could happen. She tried not to think about how sick she felt, too. A baby was coming.

Every day the wheat grew higher. The feathery tops waved gently.

One afternoon Laura went to her window. The sky had a peculiar greenish color. In the distance were dark clouds. She caught her breath.

Suddenly the storm was on them. Hail fell, huge hard balls of ice, some larger than eggs. Twenty minutes later it was over. The wheat was gone, pounded into the earth and flattened. Heartbroken, Manly told Laura, "The rich get their ice in the summer. The poor get theirs in the winter."

That fall their baby, a girl, was born. They named her Rose after the wild roses that grew on the prairie, Laura's favorite flowers. Rose would change their luck; Laura was sure of it. She and Manly felt happy again.

Each year was harder, though. Hot, dry weather had come to South Dakota. The wind blew over the wheat, cooking it before it had grown to full size. "How heartbreaking it was to watch the grain we had sown with such high hopes wither and yellow in the hot winds!" Laura said.

She and Manly were terribly sick with diphtheria. They were both tired, worn out. Manly would have to walk with a cane for the rest of his life.

In August 1889 Laura had another baby, this time a lovely little boy who looked like Manly. Days later he died in her arms, still unnamed. Laura wondered if they'd ever be happy again.

It seemed as if things couldn't get worse. They tried to carry on, wondering how they'd pay the debts that were growing larger all the time.

Then something else did happen. One day Laura

went into the kitchen and started the stove. When she went into the other room to sweep, she heard a rustling sound.

It was the sound of fire.

She raced back to the kitchen, but by now the whole room was on fire. The roof caught, and by the time help arrived, the house was gone.

Manly found Laura sprawled across the horseshoe-shaped driveway, sobbing, wondering if he'd ever forgive her.

The first years were over, hard, terrible times for farming. Yet, "We'll always be farmers," Laura said.

Somehow they'd have to find a way to start over.

5

On the Way Home

When Laura finished writing *The First Four Years* on lined copy paper, probably sometime in the 1940s, she put it away instead of sending it to her editor. No one is sure why. By that time she was close to eighty. The book was not published until 1971, fourteen years after her death.

The First Four Years was not the end of Laura's story. What happened to her next is told in the book *On the Way Home.*

Laura never meant it to be a book. It was simply a diary about what happened that summer of 1894. She tucked the five-cent notebook away in the attic of Rocky Ridge Farm.

Years later her daughter, Rose Wilder Lane, found it. By this time, Rose was grown up and a writer herself.

How well she remembered the trip from South Dakota to Mansfield, Missouri, when she was seven years old. She could still picture her mother writing in the little notebook as they jogged along in the wagon, in the summer's heat.

Rose wrote an introduction and an ending to the diary. She wanted to tell more about Laura and Manly . . . how they got ready for the trip . . . and how they found the farm when the trip was over. Then she sent it off to Laura's publisher. This new book, *On the Way Home,* would answer children's questions about what happened next to Laura, how she and Manly started over.

Early in the morning of July 17, 1884, Laura hugged Ma and Pa and her sisters, wondering how soon, if ever, she'd see those dear faces again.

The wagon was ready. Everything they owned was packed carefully for the long trip. There were pots and pans and beds and clothing. Even the chicken coop was attached to the back, with the hens clucking and ruffling their feathers.

Most important was what was hidden away in the writing case Manly had made for her. It was the money that would change their whole lives—money to buy a farm in Missouri.

How hard Laura had worked for that hundred-dollar bill! She had spent a hundred days in the dressmaker's shop cutting buttonholes, making seams, hemming shirts. Every morning except Sunday she had started by six and had hardly looked up from her sewing until it was time to leave at six that evening.

Now, as she climbed up on the wagon with Manly and Rose, she waved one last time to Pa and Ma. Then they were off.

Their wagon was not the only one on the road. Wagons were moving back and forth across the country. People were leaving places that were hard for them. They were driving away from farms that didn't produce enough food. Everyone hoped to find a better place.

Laura looked forward. She didn't let herself think of what might happen if the new place didn't work out. It was frightening to think about the wagons they passed that were coming back from Missouri. Those people had called across to her that the land there was rocky and hard to farm.

One morning she found a little dog on the road, starving and shaking with fear. She fed him scraps and tucked him up on her lap to make the rest of the long trip with them. Days later she wrote in her notebook, "Fido is a good watchdog. He growls at every stranger who comes to the wagon, and at night at everyone who passes."

The trip took forty-five days. At last, on August 30, she wrote, "At 11:30 we came into Mansfield in a long line of 10 . . . wagons."

Laura loved Missouri right from the first. She waited impatiently as Manly looked for a farm to buy. Days later he stumbled onto a place about one mile east of Mansfield. It was a forty-acre farm, with a small one-room log cabin.

Manly took her to see it. In her ending to *On the Way Home,* Laura's daughter Rose wrote, "My father was glowing and my mother shining. She never had talked so fast. Just what they wanted."

They prepared to move. "When he was excited," Rose wrote, "my father always held himself quiet and steady. . . . Sometimes my quick mother flew out at him, but this day she was soft and warm."

Laura began to dress. She combed her hair, which hung down to her feet, then braided it up on top of her head. She dressed in her wedding dress and her best shoes. They'd go straight to the bank. Opening the writing box, she reached for the one-hundred-dollar bill. It was gone.

Mouth dry, she took everything else out of the box—the writing paper, the envelopes, even the pens. Still, she didn't find the money.

Terrified, she asked Rose whether she had taken it to play with. She wondered if a stranger had somehow gotten into the wagon.

She and Manly stared at each other, horrified. The farm was lost to them.

Quietly, Manly went to town to see if he could find some odd jobs to tide them over, and Laura, heartsick, put on her work clothes again. How would they ever get through the winter?

It was days before she found the money. Still in the writing case, it had slipped down into a small crack.

Immediately, dressed as they were, they hitched up the horses, went to the bank, and bought the farm.

Hours later, Laura rolled up her sleeves and began to whistle. Happy, she bustled around to get the little cabin spic-and-span.

Then out of nowhere, it seemed, a stranger appeared, asking for work. Frightened, Laura reached into a pocket to hold onto her revolver.

The man was tall and as bony as Fido had been when they first saw him. He told Laura and Manly about his family in the wagon down by the creek. They hadn't eaten in three days.

So many farmers and their families were hungry.

So many of them had no place to go. Laura felt terrible for the man.

Still, she shook her head as Manly walked to the wagon. "No," she blurted out, thinking they had no money left and almost no food for Rose.

Without answering, Manly cut off a good-sized chunk of salt pork and sifted corn meal into a pail.

The next morning the man was back. From before dawn till after dusk, he cut wood with Manly. Manly went to town to sell the wagonload and returned, overjoyed. Someone had bought all the wood for fifty cents.

It was the beginning.

Together Laura and Manly cleared acre after acre, using a cross-cut saw. She was proud that they could work together as a team. They felt stronger every day as they turned over the rich dark earth and planted the seed. They built a hen house and a stable for the horses and began to plan for their own house.

How thrilling it was to see the shoots of corn, green and silky, as they came up the next summer! How wonderful to dig the potatoes and to cook the vegetables as they became ripe! Laura and Rose picked the huckleberries and ate them until their lips were stained purple. Then they sold the rest in town, along with eggs the hens had laid.

At last Laura and Manly picked the spot for their

house and began to build. Laura wanted windows, lots of them. She wanted to see this land that she was beginning to love. She hung her curtains so they didn't cover the windows. "I don't want curtains over my pictures," she said. "They're never the same for two hours together, and I like to watch them changing."

Almost every bit of the house was taken from the land. They cut a staircase out of a wide oak tree, and

one day Laura found three huge stones that would be perfect for the fireplace. Manly built bookcases and furniture, and together they kept working on the house. It would take twenty years to finish.

Each year the farm grew bigger. Rose was growing up, and Laura, busy with the hens and the planting and the work in the house, couldn't imagine being anything but a farmer's wife.

6

"Dear Children"

It was 1915. Laura was forty-eight years old. She was whizzing across the United States by train. The engine tore down the tracks, flying, it seemed, in a racing hurry to get to San Francisco.

Laura was in a hurry, too. She was going to see her daughter Rose, who was married now and a journalist working for the *Bulletin* newspaper.

How different traveling was now. Laura could remember the first time she had taken a trip. She had traveled slowly in a wagon . . . so slowly that she had had time to take long looks at the waving prairie grass, the birds, and the rabbits.

It had taken many men to build this railroad, and she could be proud that Pa had been a part of it.

Pa. It made her sad to think he had been dead for thirteen years now. She remembered the afternoon he had died in his house in De Smet. She had been there with him to say good-bye, to comfort Ma, and to bury him in the little prairie cemetery next to her own baby.

Pa would have loved going all the way west as she was. She was glad Rose wanted to share her new city and her life with "Mama Bess," as she called her.

Too bad Manly and Inky the dog had to stay behind. Someone had to watch out for Rocky Ridge Farm, though. Dear, generous Manly had told her she must go and write about it for him.

The trip to San Francisco would give Laura a whole new world of things to see. She wrote back to Manly about her first sight of the Pacific Ocean. "The water is such a deep wonderful blue and the sound of the waves breaking on the beach and their whisper as they flow back is something to dream about."

She was writing word pictures to Manly just as she had to Mary, and just as she would years later when she'd write her *Little House* books.

Manly must have enjoyed her letters. They were found years later, kept carefully together and tied with grocery string. They became Laura's last book, *West*

from Home, published in 1975.

Something else had happened during that trip to visit Rose. Rose put a little seed of thought into Laura's head. A writer herself, she wanted her mother to write more.

Laura did write. For the Missouri newspaper she wrote about the fair she had seen in San Francisco. She included recipes. For the next several years she wrote for other newspapers and magazines. She even had a column of her own, called "As a Farm Woman Thinks," in the *Missouri Ruralist.*

Just when she and Manly thought it was about time for them to retire and rest, something else exciting and wonderful happened. It was, of course, the years of writing the *Little House* books and learning that

children all over America loved her and her books.

In between her ordinary work on the farm, Laura visited libraries. When children wrote to tell her how they felt about her, she wrote back.

"Dear Children," she wrote to one sixth-grade class, "It is not things you have that make you happy. It is love and kindness and helping each other and just plain being good."

She told about her family in her letters, explaining that Mary had stayed with Ma—sewing, helping in the house, and going to church. Carrie had moved to the Black Hills of Dakota when she was married. Grace, like Laura, had been a farmer's wife. Now Laura was the only one still alive.

Sadly, Almanzo would die in 1949, a man of ninety-two, a man she had known and loved for almost seventy years. She told people she was so lonely for him that she could hardly bear it.

How sad it was for her. All those dear faces were gone. Only Rose was left.

People all over the country felt that she belonged to them. They honored her by naming libraries for her. She wrote to one library group: "You make good use of your library, I am sure. How I would have loved it when I was young, but I was far from a library in those days."

In 1954 Laura received a very special honor. An award was named for her. The Laura Ingalls Wilder Award is given every three years to a children's author whose books are wonderful and loved by children.

Laura was close to ninety then. She stayed quietly at Rocky Ridge Farm, making lace and quilts the way Ma had taught her. She still had visitors, friends from Mansfield and from all over the country. She said, "Sometimes reader-friends knocked on [my] door as early as seven in the morning."

It was a time for Laura to think back, to remember her long life. She could remember a time when there was no electricity, no running water, no radios, and no television.

She had lived to see the invention of cars, and the

building of railroad tracks that stretched from one end of the country to the other. Now people were even flying all over the world.

How Pa would have loved all of it. How surprised Ma would have been.

Laura's heart was failing. She had spent long, lonely days in the hospital waiting to go home to Rocky Ridge. At last the doctors realized there wasn't much more they could do for her. They let her go back to the farm.

It was 1957. February again. So long ago the trees had guarded the little house in the big woods of Pepin, Wisconsin, when Ma and Pa had waited for her to be born. Her ninetieth birthday came and went quietly. The old days seemed more real than the new.

She could remember the covered wagons, and the long winter when she had made "cats." People didn't have the slightest idea of how to do that anymore. They didn't have to.

She could remember her dear husband, Manly, as a laughing blue-eyed boy on top of a wagon of hay. She could remember herself, whistling, her bonnet hanging down her back.

Laura died at Rocky Ridge Farm just a few days after her birthday. By this time, the children who had read her books were grown up. They were giving the *Little House* books to their own children. Her readers all over the country felt as if they had lost a friend. They thought of her as Laura with the braids and the blue eyes . . . Laura the pioneer who had gone West in a covered wagon and who had seen the country grow. They saw a girl full of mischief and courage and life.

As Laura herself said, "The *Little House* books are stories of long ago. Today our way of living and learning is easier. But the real things haven't changed."

The *Little House* books were part of my childhood, a wonderful part. I wasn't sure then that there really was a Laura. I thought perhaps that someone had made her up.

Years later, when I learned that she had truly lived, had been the pioneer girl she had written about, I felt she belonged to me. This time I read not only her children's books, but some of her newspaper articles about the farm. I read letters she had written to children. I read the words of other people who had known her. Best of all, I heard her own soft voice on tape.

Laura, the person, came alive for me as I wrote, and more, Laura the writer. I spent long evenings writing and rewriting. I wanted to make this book one she'd approve of.

It became important for me to tell children how difficult some of the times in her life really were . . . times she accepted and wrote about so matter-of-factly. I wanted children to know, too, about the parts of her life she didn't write about—the days on Rocky Ridge Farm, her long years with Manly. Most of all, I wanted to tell about the qualities of love and courage that are so apparent to us in Laura's stories.

P. R. G.